THE INFIRMARY

WICK POETRY FIRST BOOK SERIES
Maggie Anderson, Editor

Already the World
Victoria Redel   Gerald Stern, Judge

Likely
Lisa Coffman   Alicia Suskin Ostriker, Judge

Intended Place
Rosemary Willey   Yusef Komunyakaa, Judge

The Apprentice of Fever
Richard Tayson   Marilyn Hacker, Judge

Beyond the Velvet Curtain
Karen Kovacik   Henry Taylor, Judge

The Gospel of Barbecue
Honorée Fanonne Jeffers   Lucille Clifton, Judge

Paper Cathedrals
Morri Creech   Li-Young Lee, Judge

Back Through Interruption
Kate Northrop   Lynn Emanuel, Judge

The Drowned Girl
Eve Alexandra   C. K. Williams, Judge

Rooms and Fields: Dramatic
Monologues from the War in Bosnia
Lee Peterson   Jean Valentine, Judge

Trying to Speak
Anele Rubin   Philip Levine, Judge

Intaglio
Ariana-Sophia M. Kartsonis   Eleanor Wilner, Judge

Constituents of Matter
Anna Leahy   Alberto Ríos, Judge

Far from Algiers
Djelloul Marbrook   Toi Derricotte, Judge

The Infirmary
Edward Micus   Stephen Dunn, Judge

The Infirmary

Poems by

Edward Micus

The Kent State University Press

Kent, Ohio

For Edjie

© 2009 by Edward Micus
Library of Congress Catalog Card Number 2009017265
ISBN 978-1-60635-035-5

Manufactured in the United States of America

The Wick Poetry Series is sponsored by the Stan and Tom Wick Poetry Center
and the Department of English at Kent State University.

Library of Congress Cataloging-in-Publication Data

Micus, Edward.
   The infirmary : poems / by Edward Micus.
      p. cm. — (Wick poetry first book series)
   ISBN 978-1-60635-035-5 (pbk. : alk. paper)∞
   I. Title.
   PS3613.I358I54 2009
   811′.6—dc22

                           2009017265

British Library Cataloging-in-Publication data are available.

13 12 11 10 09   5 4 3 2 1

CONTENTS

ACKNOWLEDGMENTS

Grateful acknowledgment to the following periodicals and anthologies in which many of these poems appeared:

Cape Rock, Chelsea, Great River Review, Harvard Magazine, Interdisciplinary Humanities, Indiana Review, Laurel Review, Mankato Poetry Review, Midwest Quarterly, New York Quarterly, North American Review, Passages North, Poetry, Seattle Review, Seneca Review, South Dakota Review, Spoon River Quarterly, Swimming with Horses 1993, and *Verse.*

Edward Micus's *The Infirmary* is masterfully arranged and paced. Its first section is comprised of poems that have a certain midwestern charm and emphasis on the local, which appeal but do not presage the darkness and gravity that will follow and accrue. What they display, however, is one of the author's considerable strengths: a finely tuned ear. "Minnesota, March," for example, ends:

Slug-heavy, we're clumsy as thumbs.
Our teeth fatten, the whites of our eyes
have cracked. There's a static
under the skin, a castanet of bones.
Our breath rattles the teacups.

As Judge, I was faced with winnowing down a slew of finalists to a few manuscripts that would merit serious consideration. We judges tend to read rather cruelly at first. As much as we're looking for something to catch our attention, we're looking to see what can easily be excluded. Micus's manuscript had its sonics going for it and a deft handling of syntax. And increasingly I felt in the presence of a *maker* of poems, someone whose language had passed a lot of hard tests. His work bespoke a history of serious reading; there were poems behind these poems.

Iowa and Minnesota give way to Vietnam in his second section. Though I was the judge in 2008, I wouldn't have been surprised, of course, to find poems pertaining to Iraq or Afghanistan in a first book, but I was reading a soldier's poems, and they were set in Vietnam! Who is this someone, I kept wondering. His is a distant war. For how many years has he been writing these poems? And should that matter? I suspected that it did matter. That is, the poems were better for having been so long considered: *The Infirmary* is so fine and disturbing.

It's divided into four sections: "Just Visiting," "Waiting Room," "Ward 3 A," and "Lower Level Morgue." Each section has its particular integrity, and each delivers in tone and substance a different aspect of the book's title and of Micus's involvement in it. The insouciance of the first section, "Just Waiting," yields to the higher personal stakes of the second section, "The Waiting Room," which in turn yields to poems and prose pieces in section three, "Ward 3 A," about people variously damaged. In many of these we hear and see that Micus has absorbed the lyrical prose of Tim O'Brien, the verse of Richard Hugo, and, in this example, Sylvia Plath's ability to keep her language vivacious while describing what's unattractive or dark.

You've brought flowers?
Rather a rag or wrench,
something to catch in my gears.

You see there's no religion here.
My dervish whirls without a prayer.
Have a seat. I'll take the air!

I have hiccups under my skin,
these tics, little lovers,
I've married them.
    —from "Visit"

The fourth section, "Lower Level Morgue," lives up to its title. It's a nightmare told years later—a little more awful because it's recollected with poise and restraint and a daring complicity. Unlike many of the Vietnam poems written at the time of the war or shortly thereafter—poems of anger or protest—Edward Micus's poems are composed, in every sense of that word. They delineate and measure their subjects; they do not advocate or hector; they do not sentimentalize. Many of them, like "Ambush Moon" and "So We Shot," will take their places among the very best war poems.

The Infirmary is a book that keeps deepening its concerns. For all its early charm, it pretties up nothing. Yet it's not without humor, and its prose interludes are written with the same care that the poems themselves exhibit. We have before us a rarity: a mature debut, a first book of poems with time-tested virtues.

I

JUST VISITING

We are the world that won't let them weep.
—*Richard Hugo*

CROWS

Oil struck in Iowa,
your wet black skims these fields.
Dot on a fencepost *i,*
then eight upbeats to a scale on wind,
the check in a kid's crayon
at two hundred feet.

Bow tie for a cornfield suit,
the groom on strung wire,
any sky beside you
makes a lovely bride.

You're the best news on the wire,
you stare down man's worst weather,
you're the pupil
in God's one good eye.

He's a little slow. Parts of him never got
done. He came late to his own litter, barely made
the doggie God cut. One third lab, one third retriever,
one-third slow. His color can't make up
its mind. Wherever it is black and brown meet

to say howdy, that place is Norton. One front leg goes
its own way but hardly knows where. A cowlick runs
the back of his neck, ridgeline fur that defies
hand or brush. It says, "It's me. It's Norton."
Norton can camp out in his own skin.

He'd go out in a storm, never know to come in. You'd find
him frozen, a stiffened tail or an ear flapping
out of the drift, a kind of handle Norton would leave
you. Or he'd swim after ducks until he was spent, go down
for the last time, that Durwood Kirby look on his face.

He's a little slow. But he's got the part right,
he does the part fine. Friend, if your grin goes bad,
if love won't keep you company, if your whole goddamn life
comes down on top of you, Norton's fault it could
never, ever be.

They made us swim naked at the YMCA. We were six or seven years old or so, dozens of us huddled along the ceramic shore, a cluster of behinds. The water was more green than blue and a haze gathered above us, a primordial mist that trapped itself beneath the ceiling canopy. They would teach us to swim, make us into little four-oared boats with peckers for rudders. But some sea in us already knew who we were and we took to water like lemmings, bumping again and again into each other, so many limbs flapping about in that little pool.

We tried to drown the weak. We squashed Leslie Morgan against the side of the pool until he hollered Uncle. We dragged Fats Logan to the murky depths and held him there, stuck rubber rings into his crack. We climbed on top of each other and fought two against two until the death or until our nuts were crushed against the necks of our partners. We crawled amphibious back to shore, slid along the slippery tile on our behinds, waving our arms and chanting the chant primeval. We stood in the warm shallows and smiled, little yellow clouds rising beside us.

"I don't understand," our mothers would say, "why they don't make them wear suits."

We knew things. We knew things our mothers might never know and those things made us stronger. Jimmie Geralk had a birthmark on his ass, the state of Louisiana. Justin Rail had no testicles as far as we could see. On the diving board Dutchie O'Dell's pecker had a hook on the end. Tommie Anderson's hid beneath a jacket of skin. And when we straddled the rope that strung the bobbing buoys between the deep and shallow ends, riding it cowboy, one hand waving the wetgreen air, a sensation crept through our groins, half pain and half pleasure, a kind of sex.

And the animals in question—four pink-eared, black-and-white
    laboratory rats—
appeared to be dreaming about something very specific: the maze they
    were learning to run.

Ah, the young Neapolitans, pink and pet furry,
tails up and they're mobiles for a nursery.

When old Aunt Lizzie kept
her cold course, we veered left.

Traveling companions,
a million-year nap and we both awoke mammalian,

womby warm and breasty,
or dragging a sacful of testes.

How we scavenged, shared the same diet.
Blood and marrow, gristle and grain. Cheese or chocolate?

We can't get enough of each other. We eat
and breathe and sleep together.

It's the dream milk, cloudy with scene and circumstance.
Now day in review, the second chance.

Tomorrow the old routine, the mazes again.
Dry those red tears, old friends.

Sweet dreams, little sleepmates, and all the right turns—
tonight we'll run the learning curve.

INDUSTRY, IOWA

Roll your windows up. When the Old Fort Road
bends south to pick up Vincent, take the dust west
until the wires quit. Look for a break in the corn.
That's Industry.

Wear something worn. Tar never stole gravel
from these chickens. For a dime in '17 a pig or boy
could ride the Northern to Fort Dodge. Bad times
don't stretch pork or steel much. Now

it's weather and Sundays come here.
Wind's the oldest citizen, the elevator raises
pigeons, the only store ran out on you. Two houses
left, rough cut. The horse that dragged the lumber up

from Kelley's Creek? Stitching on some city shoe.
Nine born in one of those rooms. Woman came out
to sweep the porch, half the town was gone. Two graves
around back, pines for stones. It's seven miles

to Vincent, take your guess about the graves along the way. You'll get
an honest look, three fingers of whiskey, overalls if the sky's thinking,
if that decision's wet. Sleeping or drinking's better
with a rain than with a woman. Take in what

you like. Don't buy a stranger a drink if your vowels
aren't right, and don't bring up Industry. Here men
do their drinking, their living, straight ahead.
They don't look sideways like you.

(for Ruth Ann Flattery)

Paper or plastic won't do.
Testes bagged double
can only mean trouble
if the sac should break through.

Steel's no better.
If your oil dries up
the housing will crack
and the bearings will turn unspeakably blue.

A little compartment
of balsa and glue?
Light in the crotch
but the slivers, *ach du!*

Or a pocket of denim,
pre-wrinkled and blue.
In one generation you'll fall out of fashion
and your knees might wear through.

Make mine a kind of basketball rind,
a shanty of skin from my crocodile kin,
tooled and pebbled and seamed in the middle—
two rooms with a spectacular view.

DANNY'S BAR

One step in the door, you know. The place
you're looking for. Last week's smoke, clots of
yellow light and yellow beer, weather
for the eye and throat.

Four old-timers in a corner playing cards. One guy
can't hear. Another guy yelling in his better ear:
"Queens are dead!" Rummy brings them in at noon,
whiskey keeps them here past supper.

A drunk is sleeping on the bar or he's dead
from eating turkey gizzards. Four eggs swimming
in a jar. "No Spitting On The Floor."

Danny could be mayor.
You get the local politics or Tammy Wynette,
three for a quarter. There's local beer
and whiskey back. Every third drink's free, stranger.

The gal who lives above the bar comes down
to work at four. Her smile's good. Another whiskey
up? You'll swear you knew her once before.

By six o'clock you've lived here thirty years.
Your coin, your eyes are swimming in the mirror,
you're buying drinks for regulars
and you ask the girl if she remembers you.

MINNESOTA: MARCH

A million years at sea,
another million sunning on a stone,
now we're put up like jam,
shut up like the insane.
All winter long we've baked a flaky white.

The air has a mood, our blankets
are all gone sour. Love, if we could
sweeten them on the line,
palm the wrinkles out.

Slug-heavy, we're clumsy as thumbs.
Our teeth fatten, the whites of our eyes
have cracked. There's a static
under the skin, a castanet of bones.
Our breath rattles the teacups.

In a co-op. Off Nicollet Avenue in the middle of the block, in a co-op with a yellow awning and a canary in one window. I had only stepped in from the rain, my life clipping along just fine. This small shop, crammed with everything ever grown or dried, from avocados to herbal tea, and between the squash and new potatoes this lovely woman in an apron, holding a squash in her hand, her eyes the color of chickpeas. "OK, don't stare," my just fine life said to me, "the rain has stopped." The next day I was back and went up to her and said, "Some of these, please," and held open the bag while she scooped them in. I still have that first pound of lentils sitting in the dark of a cupboard somewhere, waiting for Godot. Tuesday it was cornmeal and rock salt, Wednesday a string of garlic that hung above her head. Two eggplants on Thursday to learn Thursday was her day off, that her name was Anna. And Friday she smiled me back my change and said, "Nice to see you again."

All the next week this went on. Isn't it queer how a man will go up to his neck in quicksand before he'll go up to a woman?

OK. It would be Monday then, late Monday, with a scrap of wind caught in the awning, dusk with a small hand on the glass, and she was huddled over a bin of something I didn't know the name for. When she looked at me, she brushed away the hair from her eyes with the back of her hand the way her mother did, and she was so beautiful you would love her in a very small room or in no room at all. "Anna," I said, going up to her, that word a stone for the throat, "Anna," I said, "my pantry's full."

RIDDLE

I'm a playing card dealt,
or I'm handed down, cell to mother cell,

like a recipe. I'm the spiral on the stair
and I can multiply like fingers.

This crowded room I live in—
but such windows—

a dozen billion years or more
unloading their freight at my door.

I puff, I click, I hiss,
I'm the flavor on the breath,

the best you'll ever be.
This is all love means to me:

a galaxy nurses its stars,
a billion atoms to a billion squared

meet in a fish or a flower,
a dinosaur awakens to walk on air

so I might have a word with you.

PHOTOGRAPH: BOY IN A SUIT, SIXTH GRADE

Wallets are too common, albums too comatose
for photographs. Mantels? They're for ticking
fathers. I keep this scrap of him in a corner
of the mirror. He's yellowed there,
shed the cocoon suit, felt a knuckle or two
of new wind since that year froze upon the glass.
His mother, I remember, picked the tie—
but the knot—a mystery. Simple enough
to stand behind a boy in front of a mirror
and hand some secret down. And what would ever
be more than this—the handing down I mean,
one mouth, one hand to the next, and always
the blood taking in what it can, making its laps,
leading us on.

Blood has the best memory, blood takes pictures
of its own: the shaping of stone upon stone,
the hunt, the long trek home, the fire making.
And the fathers, the terrible fathers,
blood has them all, squatting in the darks of caves,
turning their hearts on sticks.

January slaps these flatlands with an open hand.
Beneath the swirl of snow-born blur
you found a town. The map said, "Klossner, 46."
You said, "Bar and German luck."
Lines are down, power's out and in—
but the gal behind the bar
pours your whiskey up, her red hair works.
Call this home until the whiteout's done.

The farmer on the end says '17 was worse;
the redhead, '81. Your say is final, friend.
Drink to this: once the weather held in '66,
but a lover and a child went bad.

Wind and whiskey up, power's out again,
candlelight is swimming in your bourbon.
Little promise in this weather—
but how love loves a storm—
supper called the farmer home,
the red-haired gal just asked your name.

Rivers are blue for maps and children.
The Minnesota hurries run-off brown,
hauls the first of winter down to Minneopa Falls,
takes on the drop. This river isn't right. It must have been
the fall. A mile or two downstream it hangs a sudden left,
muscles north against the map. This river's lunatic.
In a wash of mist above the roll Ana sees a camel—no, a buffalo—
about to leap. Forty feet below the drop our veins crawl purple
in the soak. Ana, we're too old for this. What holds us here?
The pool? The plunge? Wet thunder? Something with the water.
We could turn to stone on stone along this bank, Ana,
we could die here.

Look again into the mist, find a face
that loves you there, it's mine. I'll meet you
here a hundred years from now, I'll say it
then, I'll shout it then above the roar,
above the din that breaking water makes,
I loved you all my life and never
said I loved you one small piece of it.
Ana, hold your hand beneath the coldness,
beneath the quickness of the water.
It will feel nothing but time and bits of time.

Frozen dawn. A scattering of snow
spits a boy raw welcome,
waiting for a bus beside the road.

Hangover moon, knuckle in a glove
worn through. A flock of geese, some
frozen. Dawn, a scattering of snow.

The sky is maverick. Clouds
are rolling black, tossing vagabond.
Waiting for a bus. Beside the road

a dozen ghosts are whining in the grove.
Ditch and stubble fields, tar that never ends;
a frozen dawn, a scattering of snow.

His breath carves little statues out of cold.
A schoolboy's a victim to this wind,
waiting for a bus beside the road.

I wave and honk the horn. Crows explode
along strung wire, flak bursting on the wind.
Frozen dawn, a scattering of snow.
Waiting for a bus beside the road.

The gal behind the bar pours her smile, your whiskey
up. Some red storm's undone her hair, but the weather
in her eyes says fair to partly intimate. Your first wet kiss,
remember it? In a meadow south of town, where the river

bends a dozen miles hard for home, you were born again
and fast, the Harley bearing witness in the grass. A laying on
of hands. Blue jeans on the handlebars, a flock
of underwear. Your world spun carnival

and sky, that girl-shaped cloud again, a swirl of river
and wind. Her kiss is mostly gone, and the Harley's
stored in your garage. But the river runs. Life's a kiss,
I'm almost sure of it. The kiss goes out and in a nebula

as far away as thought, a new star kicks its furnace
in. I'll say this, when the priest is celibate, when the sermon's
done: even stars raise their young. Let me guess Diane—the name
of the gal on the Harley, I mean. I'll guess her seventeen

and blonde with breasts you could set
your best china on. You wrote the script. Tell me
I missed it, friend. Tell me I've got it goddamn wrong
and we will absolutely go—there's no other word for it—dead-on.

(for Terry Davis)

NOTIONS

I'm out in the garage, Granny's Brown'n'Bag
around my head,

tucking my last thoughts, my wasted haircut in
(I planned a tidy getaway, the lawn and hedges trimmed, the taxes
    done)

the barrel of the gun as cool as penance against one ear,
eternity breathing into the other

and I could hear between the two of them
fifty years of gear and grind, sink and counterspin,

a steady thud of bone on bone, that old refrain.
I could see my end right through the cellophane

when down the alleyway Carnie
kicks his Harley in.

When I threw that .45 into Murphy's pond,
it bubbled up like an afterthought in some cartoon.

Won't it all come down to this—
a quasar, a quirk, a chunk of randomness,

some might have been—the kitchen phone, a gust of wind,
a fly on an oil spot, Miss Peggy calling, "Supper's done."

Or that way a winter crow, chiseled
in sleet and cold,

and so long in keeping there,
out of whim or retrospect, lifts itself above strung wire.

ARM WRESTLING

They have propped their elbows on the back table
at Maggie's Saloon, two hinges primeval,

evolved in natural rubber and bone,
a fulcrum where a billion years have swung,

and above each hinge a tattoo farm.
Now we have the hooking up, the forearms

join along a seam
it could be a kind of mating.

Two thumbs embrace to make a hitch,
then palm to palm, eight fingerhooks.

Inside each arm a band of muscles, strung
and tuned, plays the battle hymn.

A gang of nerves.
The heart shifts gears,

blood hurries along,
something triggers in the groin.

I know a woman who, if you love her enough,
will lie beside you and settle the back of her hand

along your cheek, or your temple say, with the palm
facing out, to show there is nothing in the hand,

a kind of surrender
if you like, as if you had won.

TO STEVE, AFTER READING
THE PYRAMIDS OF MALPIGHI

These are hard times, friend. Can hardly get the music in. Oh, my blood's keeping time, making its laps. It goes about, busy as thought, doing what it's supposed to. It's the old woman in me, full of spit and rumor, who sits and spins and stirs the same old pot. I may have my way with her yet. Brandy still pleases me, my gamblings. Where would we be without the dichotomy, the splits and double downs, the double helix we all play on, that mirror on the bedroom wall that will not let us in?

Yesterday a January thaw and I swear a metal rain tap-dancing on the roof. Tinsel, remember it? Tinsel. Even the sound of it makes a little bell. How we drenched the tree with it, tossing those shreds of light from our fingertips, as if that small delight would save us from ourselves and the world. This morning frost found every lawn and leaf, glass and stem. Stuck in the eye of every bird. Even my single sock, fallen from the laundry basket. I won't have it any other way—the frost, I mean, that it had beauty on its mind. I suppose we all could be singular colors, or perfectly bored in the circular. Ah—even that shape a kidney likes to make. And all those Egyptians inside!

II

WAITING ROOM

OUT OF BIEN HOA

At the Repot Depot
out of Bien Hoa

a thousand bowels American
roll in each day,

shithouses toe the tarmac,
afternoon tin splinters the eye.

McHenry and I lift the flaps,
wheel the half-barrels out.

I stir with a paddle,
he pours on the fuel oil,

lights and relights the shit.
"D'ya think you hear the bullet

if you're shot in the head?"
"I suppose," he says,

"ya hear it knocking on the door—
but when you go to answer you're not even there."

Knee-deep in the barrel,
I'm stirring, he's pouring the oil,

and I can't find the sun
for the black smoke that rolls off the pile.

ROBERTSON

Like the panties
Newman stuffed

inside his steel pot
or that rosary
Meyer wound about

his neck
Robertson kept

a ring of smoke
around his head.
Eleven months he did

Thai sticks for a dollar
through the wire

and every dawn
some fog rolled in
across the breakers in his brain.

A hot shrapnel scrap
kissed his kneecap
sent him back to Burlington.

Jesus—what a war—
to leave him hanging here

back in the world
his brain uncured
still smoking in its skin.

FIELD SOUTH OF HECTOR, MINNESOTA

Stones. The earth offers them up in her hands.
On the latest tide they arrive,
in their gray traveling suits.

Fieldstars. On the west side, a constellation—
another flurry along the fence row,
a dozen or two, elbow to elbow.

The wagon clunks, the farmer curses,
even the woman, floral bright,
is somber as a shift worker.
Is there nothing in a love for stones,
their randomness, their *how-do-you-do*s,
that lunatic grammarian in all of us
who would punctuate a field?

This one, the size of a brain,
if we could crack its quiet—
it swims with molten passions, the earliest of news.
Our phantom lives fly off,
they have no ballast, no grip.
But stones remember, and up the dark corridor,
good neighbors,
come tap-tap-tapping on our vaulted doors.

STICKS

In the late-day heat off Highway 1
an old woman from the village came up
to us with her blackened teeth, with her hands
begging, and a soldier in the platoon
shoved her face with the palm of his hand,
slammed her head to the ground, it pleased
him this way to hurt her. She picked herself up,
tugged at a new kid in back of the column
who slipped her a tin of pears.

When my own grandma turned 100,
she said, "Good enough." The farmer in her
wanted three digits, that yield.
"Mamma" was all my mother said,
those first sounds that hold hope best
for any of us. I'd say this at little risk:
We'd love a soldier or a woman most
for what that mother was.

It tires me now to think back
on Highway 1, how he held his weapon
to the woman's head, made sounds
in his mouth boys make
playing Army in an alley somewhere.

There is something that hatches
in the heat of the brain, that flaps
terribly about in the cellar
of the brain. There is something

that has no mother at all,
that if it could
would have its way with you.

WOMAN AT THE WALL

This is what she does:
she places her arm
behind the neck of the name
or around the name's shoulder,
she kisses the name on its forehead,
that way mothers do.

She prays
that tonight while she is sleeping
God will put all the names into a jar
and pull the one name out,
that in the morning when she awakens
she will find the name
sleeping again in its bed,
that she won't know any difference.

DEVIL'S ISLAND, FRENCH GUIANA

Today clouds should be criminal, dressed in penal gray,
sky shackled in slate, wind should tear the sea
into pieces. Not this pour of Atlantic blue, these counterfeit
blues that season the sky. Or the way a scarlet ibis lifts

its reds above the mangroves and palm trees turn
so suddenly with light your eye would swear
any prison here was built for irony. Even the lepers
have taken their misery to the mission at Cayenne.

Here a man was married to the dark for seven years
inside a box of stone. If another man, a kindhearted one,
had opened a crack in the western
wall that faces Kourou, half the world

might have seeped through. That sliver of sun
beneath the iron door could never save him,
the tympani of rain on stone, or whatever
flavored his mind—a sip of Merlot, a melody perhaps,

April on the Champs-Élysées, or the daughter lovely
in Bordeaux who still rocks his ghost. When he cracked
his head a dozen times against the stone but couldn't
finish it, they dragged him out, shook their heads,

tossed him back. And on the Île Royale,
a mile across the God-blue sea, when a woman
in a bamboo hut turned a certain way,
the leper who loved her called the moment grace.

SIN CITY, AN KHE

Twenty bars all named for states,
no Iowa. Try the California:
plastic fruit, painted surf, a UCLA pennant,
Beach Boys on the jukebox, and whiskey
enough to burn holes in the war.

Girls in jeans or quicker silks.
The one who sits on your knee
and calls you *babysan* can't be 17.
Without the chewing gum,
the rhinestone buckle on her belt,
you might have loved her in a book you've read.

If you never take her
past the dangling colored beads
to the upstairs room where candles burn
that flavor in her hair,
if you never touch her where you please,
only lie beside her wondering
what she and you are doing there,

you've been so dark down
in that foxhole dark that jungle dark so long
she'll still go down
on you for five dollars MPC,
she'll still pretend you didn't
burn her village to the ground,
she'll light you up like napalm.

GIRL IN NAPALM

When I came home from the war something
started in my head rolling
you know a little
ball out of round
that won't fit on
the nose of the clown and another
thing sticks in the pan
of my brain smokes black without
curls when I pray
for rain behind my eyes
there is clear weather
I mean that
I can see through
a child's skin painted yellow on
how her Lego bones
are joined and all the napalm
falling falling falling down don't
hide in the village little
one fire finds hair jelly
finds skin some
other time the girl
I wanted to love always best
gave her grown-up breasts
melted to me I guess
to my hands.

Tarmacadam sky. The one last sun you counted on
gone to bruise and residue, down
some alleyway bad weather makes.
Every cloud dissolved in tar,
that runway running pitch and poor
seven hundred miles north to Brenner Pass.
Curse the voice that called your name,
that fell 10,000 feet from here, the boulevard
of screams beneath your bomb site hair.

There's a lover tapping on your door
but you're lost fast in engine hum,
ack-ack blotting your best dream. Sky dies
hard in black on black, you die best alone.
What blue, what scrap of sky
for forty years remembered you
when dogs were sudden at your throat,
when wavering you rode that last slag home?

   (for Richard Hugo)

TRASH RECEPTACLE VOICE, KENTUCKY FRIED CHICKEN, 403 SOUTH BROAD, MANKATO, MN

"Thank you," it says, in a voice that knows
what human is, "Thank you," it says. Such politeness, you'd think
the world were right—drumsticks and thighs bobbing in fat
and dreaming salvation, chickens whole again, hearts and necks and
    gizzards
and livers soaring above Rapidan Dam on honey-glazed wings.

It's your dentist's voice under gas, the voice
of your mother that led you to sleep, your Father Confessor
in the shadow box. Drop to your knees beside the bin,
tell the flap your darkest sin.

When the black-haired boy
in the corner booth, the fish-eyed one, his brain
seventeen weeks undone, tosses his bones
into the catacombs and walks into miraculous air,
he'll find a new womb waiting there, "Thank you."

You'll be shipwrecked soon enough
up the hill at St. Joe's Immanuel with a heart that marks
three-quarter time, a liver that doesn't give a damn.
Take a final look around. No one's sitting
in the blueback chairs, no lovers or your loyal Malamute,
just a voice that winters
in your ear. And when you've thrown
your life away, "Thank you," it will say, "Thank you."

From overhead, the door gunner's 7.62 millimeter round entered the base of the boy's neck, crisscrossed the body, and blew out the rib cage even as the boy crumpled into the mountain stream that ran down the draw to the valley floor. "Chúng ta sẽ trở voề tặng nó chúng ta sẽ trở về tặng nó," one of the fleeing North Vietnamese said, but his comrades could not come back for him.

The current urged the body of the boy along until it caught upon and curled around a boulder at the edge of the water and bobbed there, in uniform NVA gray and in yellow, before the current took the yellow away and left the boy making one face then another in the moving water.

"What the fuck we got here," Tony said and waded in, pinned the head of the boy with one GI boot to the boulder top, and held the ear of the boy apart from the head, the way you hold the wing of a foul before the boning knife. The machete made a thwack, the dull note falling into the stream even as the face of the boy came apart. Tony tucked the ear into a plastic bag beneath his helmet liner where he kept a picture of his girlfriend, Patty, along with Heather, the 1964 July Playmate of the Month, then left the body of the boy for the little pool in the mountain brook.

Tony took the ear back to the world, mixed glycerin and formaldehyde in a jelly jar where the ear could live. He punched a hole in the lobe for the chain to thread through. Tony wears the ear around his neck, dangling from a copper chain, from bar to bar. When someone asks to see the thing, Tony undoes the chain and lays it on a table or bar. Sometimes he holds the ear into the ear and speaks into it, "Yellow Gook, are you listening?" Or Tony may take the finger of a pretty girl, her pinky finger, and trace with it the ridge that runs along the ear, the little place where the ear was once attached. If the finger were a pencil it would make the letter D. And once a beautiful red-haired girl with emerald eyes whispered into the ear, "Hello in there," and her giggle caught in the cradle of the ear, in its cavity, if only for a moment or two.

Don't believe this story. It's bullshit. Tony did have the boy's ear pinned to the boulder, the machete glinting in the sun above his elbow, but Sergeant Roper shouted, "Get the fuck moving. We ain't got time for that shit," and we left the NVA kid and his ears bobbing in the mountain stream.

FIREBASE RED

Six pairs of combat boots
the chaplain laid out on Firebase Red,
six pilgrims who had come that far.
When a hard rain picked at the hill
they had no sense at all,
the mother voices out of ear.

The chaplain laid his own tongue out,
and a thousand Christs danced on it
that way Christ came down
in the rain,
six boots spilling with grace
and bugle notes.

Kids these days. They're into the GI look.
Willie asks what I did with all my army stuff.
I tell him I gave away a whole
duffel bag full to Goodwill.
"Gee, that was dumb."

Not the boots.
I keep a pair in the back of my head.
They're splattered with red mud,
still perfectly good.

III

WARD 3 A

GROUP HOME VAN

Community closet
for droolers, headbangers, the fish-eyed,
the over- and the underdone.
They ride, pinned under glass,
their organs pickled in a six-doored jar.
They swim with strokes we'll never learn
in the eye of a very small god.

At the stoplight they try us on.
Should we curse them with our perfect vowels,
pan the sky for weather?
If an atom dances on a string,
takes an extra step or misses one,
we're them.

We owe them
our pink brains,
muscles strung and tuned,
the way our shoulders turn for grace,
the gardens in our groins.

MASTECTOMY

My phantom nipple feels a chill
And if I itch, I scratch the air.

Through this haze of Demerol, the neon whites,
I see my firstborn nursing there.

When the father ran off, ta-ta,
I uncorked the Cabernet.

But you, you, dear friend,
How very far we've come.

And always the heart beneath you, doing its two-step.
For fifty years we've danced to it.

All right, I'll admit,
You were always my favorite—

I'd rather they'd taken the other.
Now my heartbeat rattles the air.

I'm a one-eyed Jill,
A Twiddle-Dee-Dum,

A dromedary.
Such a vacancy you leave,

A puddle of shadow, an abandoned lot.
Are you sorry, sorry?

Oh, they'll replace you soon enough with a plastic tent,
Or a saline bubble with a rubber nipple.

But you know how I'll keep on. I'm hardly undone.
I'll still sail half-mast, old friend,

on this sweet breath you've left me.

(for Miss Peggy)

ME AND MCCARV

Me and McCarv when we was ten,
shootin' craps behind the church
instead of goin' in,
laying the 2 to 1 craps ain't no sin.

Twenty years since then
he's haulin' bread at 4 A.M.
and some goddamn semi in front of him
splatters his brains with a chunk of iron.

I drive to Des Moines to see him.
Doc's making hope 1000 to 1,
he's sure as shit
McCarv's a bedpan idiot.

Me and McCarv's
shootin' craps and drinkin' beer
and he's rollin' them bones
in his one good ear

and talkin' outta
the side of his mouth,
"Comin' out, I'm comin' out,"
and I gotta fiver here

says you can't piss a drop
and he rolls Little Joe
back to back and I says
"You're so goddamn hot, McCarv."

SCHIZOPHRENIC

Split? Like a chromosome,
or a lizard's tongue? Ha!
I'm more than myself, I'm added on.

Bad mother, they used to say.
And Uncle Billie's babbling under stone,
with his *da-da*s, his *how-do-you-do*s.

They're after me all right, this posse of smocks.
They'd have my sperm on a slide,
my brain in a box.

It's the voices, you see.
I raise them in the back,
a kind of nursery.

Well, this one stutters a bit.
I may have overwatered it. But all my other dears
winter nicely in my ear.

Now we have the taking of a pill.
Which do you please? The red has a mood,
makes a pretty sleep. But the white,

bossy tablet, has an awful voice in it.
Godless and watery,
it tells the others to never love me.

Her hand on my wrist awakened me—1, 2, 3, 4—my pulse at her finger-tips, then her fingertips were between the gauze and my flesh, her other hand at my back. "Try to sit up," she said. "There. Now cough."

I looked down at the layers of bandage wrapped around my middle. Cough. The sound of the word sent shock waves up from my abdomen. I managed what I hoped would pass for a cough—a wheeze, perhaps. "No," she said, "that will not do. Now cough." She pointed across the ward of the Second Surgical Hospital where an orderly, big as Kansas, was operating a kind of giant Shop-Vac machine, running its hoses down the nose and throat of a soldier who was convulsing so wildly you'd think his lungs were being sucked out of him. I coughed.

"Good," she said. "Tomorrow we'll cough again."

Yes. Let us cough again. She walked back across the ward of the Second Surgical Hospital. Later she returned, turned me gently, and slipped a syringe of Demerol into my hip. All night long I flew on the wings of her hands.

There were three things, really, those next few weeks—the fact I was alive, the fact of the Demerol, and the fact of her. We had the coughing and the changing of the dressings and the arrangement of the tubes so a thick brown-black liquid could flow freely from my side into a glass bottle, that kind you see on office watercoolers. We had the listening at the wrist, the tapping at the veins. Often she moistened my lips with a piece of damp gauze. When she did speak, she spoke efficiently, her words like little soldiers. "There," she would say. Or, "That's good. That's better." And she kept her eyes almost always to herself.

Once in the evening she came, put her fingers, sweet with water, to my mouth, and told me her name. On another day, a Sunday I think, she came in blue jeans and a khaki shirt, disconnected me, and helped Kansas hoist me into a wheelchair. She rolled me out through the ward, across a wooden walkway onto a beach, spread a blanket on the sand, and sat down beside me. The air was mild and saturated with spray. We looked out across the South China Sea.

"Tomorrow," she said, "you're going to Japan. You'll be home for Christmas."

I think I was stupid with dope. I didn't say anything. I sat on the sand like a goddamn dune, as if some word or two would have blown me away.

"Don't write," she said. Then she kissed me on the mouth and left me there.

Weren't they all beautiful, the beautiful nurses, and didn't we love them all, and those hundreds before us, with our wounds, our Demerol hearts? She was so young. I think of her now—twenty-five years later. War or no more—Christ—won't truth have its way with this: we'd love that one the best we never came to know.

They've brought in light, boiled in tubes. Ceilings
and walls, tiles and sheets, a dozen whites distill
the eye. Only my flesh can compete. The nurses sail
upstream and down in their windcaps, and soon an avalanche
of smocks, with faces cloudy as the diagnosis:
"Here, blood makes a spot. The abdomen still pouts."
Last year they took away an ovary. Troubled friend,
she swims in a glass jar in the basement. And my liver,
old soup pot crowded with leftovers. It makes
bad broth. I've sautéed it in cheap gin, the juice
from two husbands. Christ, they'll wrap it up in bacon!

The peppermint girl sponges me off. Breast by breast,
limb by limb ("The woman in 17 B is having her nipples redone"),
and saves the crotch for last. Now the priest rides in
on little smiles. I love him for his blacks, they do well
on him. I'll confess—every night I take him in
with Demerol—a kind of communion. His touch will be the last,
his fingers greasy on my lips. This death part I rehearse,
I rehearse—I think I'm getting the hang of it.

VISIT

You've brought flowers?
Rather a rag or a wrench,
something to catch in my gears.

You can see there's no religion here.
My dervish whirls without a prayer.
Have a seat. I'll take the air!

I have hiccups under my skin,
these tics, little lovers,
I've married them.

What might my fingers be?
Women buying yard goods
or Catholics at beads.

This other hand's a kind of a claw
caught in a vise.
I'm one side fire, one side ice!

See how my faces swim?
That current's always in.
Look! I'm upstream again.

I'll do 1,000 RPMs
plugged in like this.
I'm the latest Sisyphus.

The daffodils will mind themselves,
they'll behave,
they're hardly in the way.

Their yellows calm the air,
make such a quiet.
Yellow peace, I would close my mouth on it.

(for Leonard, Post-Encephalitic)

Because the woman was of your age and lovely as any of us, and had
little notion of the rebel cause or coup, her thoughts mostly with her
son, the four-year-old, where he might be, if they would force him to
put the revolver to her head, something she'd heard it occasioned them
to do, to make a point you see, and because the hand of the soldier that
held the iron prod was so much like mine or even yours, and that gentle
way he held it, the way you hold a brush to a canvas say, the poker a
good deal longer, though, and the tip of the poker unspeakably red, and
how he drew it across her breasts, across her nipples, first one, then the
other, so the thing might have been the finger of a child or a lover, each
nipple for one moment making a little glow of its own, then a circle of
smoke, the pulses of smoke steaming from each of her breasts, a cloudy
milk rising that was not milk at all, and how her screaming led him on,
so that he teased her a bit here and there with the poker thing, some-
thing he liked to do, as if it might find a little secret somewhere for his
general, as if his life might be better somehow for what he did to her.
All I want to say is that I love you terribly because of it; how it pleases
him I mean to do this. And when pain takes away the senses of this
one, he will ask for the other, a younger girl with long dark hair, her
nipples the color of plums, and those little places in her so very, very
red he will think she could be burning there already.

INSOMNIAC

All night long these minutes,
a mob of idiots,
babbling to themselves.
It's my heartbeat sets them off,
my accordion breathing.
In twos and threes they twirl and waltz,
in their roundabout feet.
Such piles of footprints they leave,
a blackened confetti.
All night long breeding
on their half-planets,
the dark side of the eye.

What time is it?
Some ratchet's got hold of me.
I turn like a four-edged nut,
side to side, back to front.
I tighten and loosen, loosen and tighten.
Is that a crumb of daylight on the sill?

Oh, I have pills all right,
reds and whites
as pretty as dawn.
They make an hourglass.
It turns around and around.
Red side up, red side down,
all night I keep filling it with sand.

IV

LOWER LEVEL MORGUE

M-16 ROUND

Little gymnast, how you spin,
how the flesh applauds
when you tumble in,
ricochet off bone,
you're a perfect ten.

One blink in an ambushed eye
and you're already there.
You're the quiet
in the dead boy's ear.

There was a quiet knuckle on the door. And the deputy sheriff in his silver and browns, standing in the doorway with his death face on, so that the doorway made a picture frame. "Gretchen Nolan?" he asked her. He was too small for the wide-brimmed hat. He took off the thing and held it in his palms as if it were a gift and asked again because he needed to be sure. "Your son is Charles Nolan?" "I already know," is what she said and she began the walk for the dead, making one death loop then another, through the kitchen and the living room, past the floral couch and the Kelvinator, because she could not do any other thing. The deputy took a step inside. "Are you all right? Mrs. Nolan, maybe we should go." "Yes, I suppose. Should I take my purse? For what?" she thought. "But maybe then I should." "Charles," she said in the back of the squad. She chanted it a hundred times because she could not stop the word from swinging on a tire in her head.

Mr. Grady owned the dead, the dead were his. He led her across the burgundy rug, what color's death she said then down the linoleum stairs to the holding place and peeled the sheet slowly away from the boy, the way you peel the paper from the back of a stamp. His hands were not right, laid crisscross upon his lap; he never held his hands that way. She smoothed his hair and kissed him on an eye and pressed her cheek against his own and Mr. Grady pulled the sheet back over the boy so there were only four of them: Mr. Grady, the mother and the boy, and the other thing the mother had become.

AMBUSH MOON

The moon has a mood,
the moon has its bad face on.
We slip down

the draw to the valley floor,
circle the village.
In the hooches

there is a place for
a fire and small god to live.
Children

are sleeping their sleep
on straw mats and they are
beautiful in their yellows and blacks.

They are beautiful,
they are sleeping,
let us wake them.

We have come
12,000 miles
to find them.

They are beautiful,
they are sleeping oh
the moon
has a mood
the moon has something
to do.

PICTURE STORY: AUSCHWITZ

She's seven, as pretty as any to come off the train,
in her cotton pinafore, the kind that mothers make.
She's seven, in September say, on a Sunday why not
when a hard wind comes out of the north
and shudders the camp, when there are voices
in the wire and God has made them.

You would have the commandant, the one
with the swagger stick step up and say,
"Go home, all of you; we have something better to do,"
you would have the sun break out
so suddenly, like an inmate from an asylum,
that even the soldiers who herd the children,
who hurry home to stroke their children, that even the guards
who sort teeth look up from their piles.

It's just a little joke
September plays, and she is led off anyway.
You have this photograph of a girl of seven
in a pinafore by a train in September say,
on a Sunday why not. Bury her face
deep in your face. Here is the blessing
she leaves for you—a kind of gift—you never knew her,
couldn't really love her. This lovely smoke
she makes, never sister, never daughter.

CANOPY

There is that dark undone
from your woman's hair that flavors a room,
another dark that rinses hours from the eye,
the mother dark we carry in our hands,
an older dark that tunnels through subway bone,
dark of the brain before the storm.

We laid nine boys out
in jungle dark, we did that
in the Highlands somewhere and fumbled
with our hands to keep their limbs military.
Better that pile it pleased them once as boys to make.

If I took the one,
set him on my knee,
worked the mouth,
made him dance,
would that routine do as much for us
this night or that?
Peel the canopy back—
a billion idiot stars to a billion squared,
each tittering with light.

When she came to it, at the very moment perhaps, of his dying, on the muddy slope of a hill there would never be a name for, or when it came to her—small difference for mother or boy—she picked his T-shirt from the rag pile, soft from the washings, her foldings. She had shrunk it somehow, she remembered that, she had left it too long in the dryer, preoccupied as she had been with one thing or another. But she knew, there was no question about that. Before the telephone call, before the awful yellow telegram, before death peeked out the little window—she knew.

The officer was up the walkway now, carrying his hat in his hands. She rushed to the front porch and latched the screen to keep him out and gestured with her hand, with her palm to stop him. When he paused—then started up the steps at her again she waved him away with the rag, she drove him off with that. You'd think she was shaking it out there on the porch, those little clouds of dust it made.

It was the daughter who found her in the boy's room, the dust rag still in her hand. She had the bed, the chair and desk, his pine dresser, she had them all to do. She was at the top of the dresser, making large sweeping circles with the rag, then smaller tighter ones, first against the grain, then back again and again, turning the rag over and over in her hand, making the large sweeping circles, then the smaller ones, so that her dusting might never be done. It was the daughter who went up to her and said, "That's good, Mother, that's good enough," and took the thing finally from her hand.

NOT RIGHT

What did I know, what did I know,
of love's austere and lonely offices.
    —ROBERT HAYDEN

It was the mother, after the viewing, who said
he wasn't right. "His hair's wrong and his face,
so terribly gray." The youngest daughter
gathered her scissors and combs and things and most
of what she knew of love to carry back

to him. Mr. Hughes was in as he was always in. When she showed
him the brushes in her hand and asked for the permission
he turned away from her, as if she might hurt him somehow.
"Certainly," he said to her, "you know the way." She laid
them out: the cosmetic brush, a smaller softer one,

her scissors and combs, compacts and blushes, and because
it seemed to her there was no other place
for them, on the breast of the boy, beside a row of ribbons where
beneath the military green the bullet may have very well
gone in. How blonde he had become. Too much sun

she thought, and from above the ear she drew
a length of hair between two fingers, held the strands away
from the face, so as not to smudge his cheek or temple with the back
of her hand and trimmed the very ends and then
again, bits of blonde fluttering about the casket, the thinning
scissors all the while making its clickety-clicks. She did
the other side and leaned across the open hatch to look
at him, to see the sides were right and started on the top, carefully,
because she knew the hair was still alive. She lifted his head
from the satin pillow to tuck the hair behind. Satin. All his life

he'd slept on cotton, pillows lined with stripes—the
penitentiary kind—and never could he keep
the pillowcase on, the way he flopped about, dreaming
his boy dreams. She dabbed at his face with a Kleenex and a color
came away, an awful rose. When she rubbed a bit of cream

into his cheek with the tips of her fingers, it made
a little cloud, a kind of weather for his cheek that she worked in
to make the circle widen, then did the nose, the chin, the forehead,
and, gently, the lids of the eyes. She might have been a priest
or lover. What was the last thing that came to him

before the blackout? Half circles of hair had settled
on his cheeks, the khaki shirt, the uniform that held
him in. She blew across his face
and leaned close to him so she might
whisper it: "There is nothing more for me to do."

SCATTER HIS ASH

Where the Minnesota runs boy-hard and driven,
muscles north against sea and map,
where elms huddle derelict along the banks
and wind tears the sky into pieces,

on the breath of a boy,
along the arc a hawk makes rising,
through the downglide,
groomed by wind and memory,

in the tomb of the bulb, crocus, or iris,
in those long corridors of dark,
on the pulse of evening tide
that marks a life in one-quarter time,

on the bones of the brothers,
that bridge he has too soon crossed over,
on the bones of the father, shabby altar,
on the bones of the father.

BOY IN A RICE PADDY, HEAD SHOT

Tornado tip, small surprise of an O
led in an inch above the target eye,
eggshell skullback blown away,
his yolk running.

A medivac hinges in on metal babble,
its blades thrash the too late air
like a frantic mother.
The red cross is hysterical,
a scream painted on,
it is the prayer of an idiot.

A boy weighs most when he's fresh dead.
We hoist him in,
the door gunner asking, "Only one?"

Paddy mud will heal,
and the smile on the sniper's lip.
Small herd driven,
we're nudged along the paddy rice
by some dull prodding,
our balls small pistons.

SO WE SHOT

We liked to shoot things. Boys being boys. We shot flying and crawling things and swimming and walking things. We shot birds and parrots and gulls and beautiful things we didn't know the names for. We shot monkeys and gibbons and lemurs and deer and pigs and dogs and turtles. We shot oxen and water buffalo in the rice paddies and bet how many M-16 rounds it would take to buckle one to its knees because it was big and stupid. We shot tigers and elephants. Because we rarely saw them, we rarely shot the enemy. We shot Vietnamese women and children in their yellows and blacks and a goodly number of old men. And if any of that were not enough, we shot each other. Then we went home and shot ourselves.

WAKE

One heavy breath and I'm smudged.
They've powdered me silly! This rouge,

you'd think the color did me in.
Three days from Da Nang to Des Moines,

I rose like yeast.
They punctured me

with hooks, fingery tubes.
I'm boozy through and through.

The mortician brings his smiles in.
Parasites, they do well on him.

His parlor stinks of prayer gone bad and lavender sachet.
A clicking of beads, a shuffle of crepe.

Mother? I can't pick up after myself.
Such a pile I leave, bad boy gone off:

photos. Some flag. The idiot clocks.
I'll pop up, jack-in-the-box!

Peggy, Peggy, how death sweetens you
and I'm grounded in my satin room,

my touch as starchy as these green lapels.
My breath, does it stale, is it yellow?

And the earth, full of mouths.
This fluid in me is thin as bad broth.

How long, love, before a nipple dissolves,
a cock?